See This Christ Study Guide

An Eight-Week Discussion Group Workbook

Linda Lysakowski

Copyright © 2020 Linda Lysakowski

No portions of this publication may be reproduced, distributed, transmitted, stored, performed, displayed, adapted, or used in any form or manner without prior written permission, except for certain limited noncommercial uses permitted by the United States Copyright Act, such as brief quotations embodied in critical reviews.

ISBN: 978-1-7347992-1-7

About the Author

Linda Lysakowski, ACFRE, is a well-known author in the nonfiction realm. She is one of slightly more than 100 professionals worldwide to hold the Advanced Certified Fund Raising Executive designation. Linda has trained more than 40,000 professionals in all aspects of development in Canada, Mexico, Egypt, Bermuda, and most of the United States. She has written, co-authored, or contributed to more than two dozen books for the nonprofit sector.

She is a graduate of Alvernia University in Reading, PA with a BA in theology/philosophy, banking and finance, and a minor in communications., and she completed the Lay Ecclesial Ministry Program through the Diocese of Las Vegas, NV.

Linda's first novel, *The Matriarch*, was published in 2012. In 2018, she published *The Face of Jesus* and *The Face of Jesus Study Guide*, and in 2019, *Beyond Las Vegas: Road Trips from A to Z*.

Dedication

To Father Ron Zanoni, pastor extraordinaire!

Introduction

This study guide is for churches, book clubs, and others who want to study and discuss *See This Christ,* and more deeply understand their own personal encounters with Christ and his people.

The book consists of eight chapters. This guide is likewise organized for an eight-week discussion group, following the book, chapter by chapter. It's meant to help readers understand the role of Christ in today's world and in their daily lives. It looks at the many sides of Jesus and helps us relate his life to our own.

To get the most out of this study guide, I suggest you read the entire book first, and then go back and read each chapter, as you work through the study guide. Answer the questions on your own, and then discuss in a group your answers. And listen with an open heart to the views of the others in your group.

Discussion at this level is best held in groups of from four to eight, so if you have a large group, you may want to form breakout groups and then have each group summarize their discussion for the entire group. You can switch the breakout groups for each lesson, affording each member of the larger group a wide array of thoughts and insights.

You can also use this guide for your own personal study.

Feel free to contact me with your insights and ideas at Linda@LindaLysakowski.com or www.LindaLysakowski.com.

Week One: The Laughing Christ

See this Christ who is laughing,
and dancing with the children in the streets.

Jesus answered, "How can the guests of the bridegroom mourn while he is with them? The time will come when the bridegroom will be taken from them; then they will fast.

After reading The Laughing Christ, what insights did you gain?

_____
_____
_____

Answer these questions:

When have you laughed with children recently and how did it make you feel?

_____
_____
_____

Do you have a hard time relating to a human, joyous, laughing Jesus? Do you relate better with the sorrowful, suffering Jesus?

_____
_____
_____

When have you used laughter to help you cope with a hard time?

_____
_____
_____

What makes you laugh or "dance the happy dance?" Can you picture yourself dancing with "The Lord of the Dance?"

_____
_____
_____

To prepare for next week:

- ◆ Read one of the stories of the laughing, dancing Jesus again, and see if you have a different perspective on the story than you had before.
- ◆ Look for the Christ in the young people you encounter this week.
- ◆ Read Chapter Two.

Week Two: The Teaching Christ

See this Christ who is teaching,
and longing for all people to be free.

Blessed are those who are spiritually needy. The reign of God belongs to them.

Blessed are those who are sad. They will be comforted.

Blessed are those who are free of pride. They will be given the earth.

Blessed are those who are hungry and thirsty for what is right. They will be filled.

Blessed are those who show mercy. They will be shown mercy.

Blessed are those who are pure of heart. They will see God.

Blessed are those who make peace. They will be called sons and daughters of God.

Blessed are those who suffer for doing what is right. The reign of God belongs to them.

What experiences and thoughts did you reflect on during the past week?

_____
_____
_____

Answer these questions:

Why do you think Jesus taught in parables?

_____
_____
_____

See This Christ Study Guide: An Eight-Week Discussion Group Workbook

Which parable do you think is sending you a message, and which character in this parable do you relate to the most?

_____
_____
_____

Do you consider yourself a good storyteller? Could you relate to people better by telling your story?

_____
_____
_____

Which beatitude resonates with you the most?

_____
_____
_____

Prepare for next week:

- ◆ Read the parable with which you most identify and try to see yourself in a different character in this parable than the one with whom you usually identify.
- ◆ Try to live out one of the Beatitudes.
- ◆ Read Chapter Three.

Week Three: The Angry Christ

The Angry Christ
See this Christ who is angry
at the way we have denied our Creator's love.

Jesus made a whip from some ropes and chased them all out of the temple. He drove out the sheep and cattle, scattered the money changers' coins over the floor, and turned over their tables. Then, going over to the people who sold doves, he told them, "Get these things out of here. Stop turning my Father's house into a marketplace!" Then his disciples remembered this prophecy from the scriptures: "Passion for God's house will consume me."

What experiences and thoughts did you reflect on during the past week?
_____
_____
_____

Answer these questions:

How do you think the disciples felt when they saw the Angry Christ? Why?
_____
_____
_____

What do you think would make Christ angry if he came back today?
_____
_____
_____

See This Christ Study Guide: An Eight-Week Discussion Group Workbook

Do you get angry at injustice? What can you do about it?
_____
_____
_____

How do you feel when you get angry? What makes you angry?
_____
_____
_____

Prepare for next week:

- When you get angry, ask yourself if you are angry at injustice or because you aren't getting your way.
- Try to understand the anger others are expressing, and whether it is just or unjust.
- Read Chapter Four

Week Four: The Healing Christ

See this Christ who is touching,
healing broken bodies, broken souls.

And when Jesus entered Capernaum, a centurion came to Him, imploring Him, and saying, "Lord, my servant is lying paralyzed at home, fearfully tormented." Jesus said to him, "I will come and heal him." But the centurion said, "Lord, I am not worthy for you to come under my roof, but just say the word, and my servant will be healed." For I also am a man under authority, with soldiers under me; and I say to this one, 'Go!' and he goes, and to another, 'Come!' and he comes, and to my slave, 'Do this!' and he does it." Now when Jesus heard this, he marveled and said to those who were following, "Truly I say to you, I have not found such great faith with anyone in Israel. "I say to you that many will come from east and west, and recline at the table with Abraham, Isaac, and Jacob in the kingdom of heaven; but the sons of the kingdom will be cast out into the outer darkness; in that place there will be weeping and gnashing of teeth." And Jesus said to the centurion, "Go; it shall be done for you as you have believed." And the servant was healed that very moment.

What experiences and thoughts did you reflect on during the past week?

_____
_____
_____

Answer these questions:

Do you ever feel like you asked for healing but did not receive it? How did this make you feel?

_____
_____
_____

Do you identify with any of the people Jesus healed? Why?

Do you ever feel you are being called to be a healer? In what way?

Healing can come in many ways; how have you been healed by Christ?

Prepare for Next Week:

- Meditate on healing Christ in scriptures and from what you might need healing.
- Look for opportunities where you might bring healing to others.
- Read Chapter Five.

Week Five: The Servant Christ

See This Christ who kneels before you
washing feet of sinful people.

John 13:1-17 It was just before the Passover festival. Jesus knew that the hour had come for him to leave this world and go to the Creator. Having loved his own who were in the world, he loved them to the end. The evening meal was in progress, and the devil had already prompted Judas, the son of Simon Iscariot, to betray Jesus. Jesus knew that the Creator had put all things under his power, and that he had come from God and was returning to God; so he got up from the meal, took off his outer clothing, and wrapped a towel around his waist. After that, he poured water into a basin and began to wash his disciples' feet, drying them with the towel that was wrapped around him.

What experiences and thoughts did you reflect on during the past week?

_____
_____
_____

Answer these questions:

Have you ever been in a position where you were called to be a servant leader? How did this make you feel?

_____
_____
_____

See This Christ Study Guide: An Eight-Week Discussion Group Workbook

Why do you think it was so important that Jesus washed his disciples' feet?
_____
_____
_____

Are you more comfortable in role of the server or the served? Why do you think that is?
_____
_____
_____

How do you think Jesus felt knowing that his disciples didn't understand why he had to wash their feet?
_____
_____
_____

Prepare for Next Week:

- ◆ Read the story of the Washing of the Feet again. Picture yourself as one of the disciples and meditate on how you would have felt.
- ◆ Try to see yourself as the servant and as the served in the situations you face this week.
- ◆ Read Chapter Six.

Week Six: The Dying Christ

See this Christ who hangs here bleeding,
weeping, dying for your sins.

About three in the afternoon Jesus cried out in a loud voice, "Eli, Eli, lemasabachthani?" (which means "My God, my God, why have you forsaken me?"). When some of those standing there heard this, they said, "He's calling Elijah." Immediately one of them ran and got a sponge. He filled it with wine vinegar, put it on a staff, and offered it to Jesus to drink. The rest said, "Now leave him alone. Let's see if Elijah comes to save him." And when Jesus had cried out again in a loud voice, he gave up his spirit. At that moment the curtain of the temple was torn in two from top to bottom. The earth shook, the rocks split apart, and the tombs broke open. The bodies of many holy people who had died were raised to life. They came out of the tombs after Jesus' resurrection and went into the holy city and appeared to many people. When the centurion and those with him who were guarding Jesus saw the earthquake and all that had happened, they were terrified, and exclaimed, "Surely he was the Son of God!"

What experiences and thoughts did you reflect on during the past week?

_____
_____
_____

Answer these questions:
Have you ever been through a tough time and didn't think you deserved to suffer? How did the thought of Jesus' suffering help you through this difficult time?

_____
_____
_____

See This Christ Study Guide: An Eight-Week Discussion Group Workbook

Where do you think you would have been during the crucifixion? Why?

_____
_____
_____

Do you ever feel like perhaps you have "crucified" someone who didn't deserve it? What did you do about it?

_____
_____
_____

Are there areas in your life you feel you need to die to in order to live with Christ?

_____
_____
_____

Prepare for Next Week:

- ◆ Think about how Jesus felt, knowing he was abandoned by most of his disciples.
- ◆ Meditate on one area of your life you would like to die to.
- ◆ Read Chapter Seven.

Week Seven: The Risen Christ

See this Christ in all His glory,

risen now triumphantly.

But Mary was standing outside the tomb weeping; and so, as she wept, she stooped and looked into the tomb; and she saw two angels in white sitting, one at the head and one at the feet, where the body of Jesus had been lying. And they said to her, "Woman, why are you weeping?" She said to them, "Because they have taken away my Lord, and I do not know where they have laid him." When she had said this, she turned around and saw Jesus standing there, and did not know that it was Jesus. Jesus said to her, "Woman, why are you weeping? Whom are you seeking" Supposing him to be the gardener, she said to him, "Sir, if you have carried him away, tell me where you have laid him, and I will take him away." Jesus said to her, "Mary!" She turned and said to Him in Hebrew, "Rabboni!" (which means, Teacher). Jesus said to her, "Stop clinging to me, for I have not yet ascended to the Creator; but go to my brothers and say to them, 'I ascend to my Creator and your Creator, and my God and your God.'" Mary Magdalene came, announcing to the disciples, "I have seen the Lord," and that he had said these things to her.

What experiences and thoughts did you reflect on during the past week?

_____
_____
_____

Answer these questions:

Do you relate more to Peter, John, or Mary Magdalen at the empty tomb?

_____
_____
_____

See This Christ Study Guide: An Eight-Week Discussion Group Workbook

Do you feel the Risen Christ working in your life?
_____
_____
_____

Do you feel the Risen Christ has come to everyone? How?
_____
_____
_____

Where do you see signs that "This is Jesus Christ, King of the Jews?"
_____
_____
_____

Prepare for Next Week:

- ◆ Try to imagine what you would have done if you experienced the Risen Christ on that first Easter Day.
- ◆ Try to see the Risen Christ in the "centurions," the "executioners" of our day.
- ◆ Read Chapter Eight.

Week Eight: The Loving Christ

See this Christ who loves you,
and wants you to be with him every day.
Yes, he wants you to be with him in all ways.
Every day.

This is my commandment, that you love one another, just as I have loved you. "Greater love has no one than this, that one lay down his life for his friends. You are my friends if you do what I command you. No longer do I call you slaves, for the slave does not know what his master is doing; but I have called you friends, for all things that I have heard from my Creator I have made known to you. You did not choose me but I chose you, and appointed you that you would go and bear fruit, and that your fruit would remain, so that whatever you ask of the Creator in my name the Creator may give to you. This I command you, that you love one another.

What experiences and thoughts did you reflect on during the past week?
_____
_____
_____

Answer these questions:

How do you think you would have answered Jesus' question, "Peter, do you love me?"
_____
_____
_____

See This Christ Study Guide: An Eight-Week Discussion Group Workbook

Do you have difficulty loving your neighbor as yourself? Which is harder?

_____
_____
_____

Do you see the Body of Christ in yourself? In others?

_____
_____
_____

Do you agree with Dorothy Day, that *"I really only love God as much as I love the person I love the least?"*

_____
_____
_____

How do you come to know Christ?

_____
_____
_____

Prepare for the rest of your life:

- ◆ Try to identify with all the images of Christ you see—laughing, teaching, angry (in a just way), healing, servant, dying (to sin), rising, and loving.
- ◆ Try to *See This Christ* everyone you meet. Yes, *everyone!*
- ◆ Love your neighbor as yourself.